STANDING
ON THE WALL

PRAYERS TO PRESERVE THE
INTEGRITY OF A NATION

I0418331

PEOPLE'S EDITION

ENDORSEMENTS

We must always stand firm, is the lesson derived from Dr. Jannah Scott's inspiring book, Standing on the Wall, *which further evidences our commitment to search for truths.*

Dr. Terry Lee, CEO
White House Prayer for our Nation, Inc.

I am honored to endorse with great enthusiasm, Standing on the Wall: Prayers to Preserve the Integrity of a Nation *by Dr. Jannah Scott. She is one of God's most humble handiworks in the high places of government, marketplace and faith based communities; making prayer palpable for the Intercessor, Statesman and the Church. These strategic prayer books will transform anyone who has a heart for America or any nation to see the Kingdom of God come and God's will be done in the earth."*

Bishop Dr. Jackie L. Green
JGM Enternational Prayer Life Institute
Redlands, CA

There is power in every prayer in Dr. Jannah Scott's book. Prophetic praying is God's tool for people of faith to preserve the integrity of the USA during these challenging times. This book's scope is comprehensive and holistic, while being intimately personal. It's worth the read . . . again and again.

Dr. Warren H. Stewart, Sr.
Chair, Arizona African American
Christian Clergy Coalition

Jannah Scott has given the people of God a clarion call to pray. The strength of this book is in its design. It is a functional prayer tool. Open this book! Pray these prayers, so the power of God may manifest in our Nation.

Tyler Johnson
Lead Pastor of Redemption AZ

STANDING ON THE WALL
PRAYERS TO PRESERVE THE INTEGRITY OF A NATION

ISBN: 978-0-9997662-3-1

10 9 8 7 6 5 4 3 2 1

All Scripture quotations, unless otherwise indicated, are taken from the New King James Version®. Copyright © 1982 by Thomas Nelson. Used by permission. All rights reserved.

Printed in the United States of America

Library of Congress Control Number: 2019916899

Author: Dr. Jannah Scott

Contributors: Cathy Fontenot and Baiyina Abdas

Edited by: Fiesta Publishing

Cover Design and Interior Layout: Alli Masi

Cover Photo: Brumidi Corridor, Senate Wing 1st Floor, US Capitol

Fiesta
Publishing
Fiesta Publishing
fiestapublishing.com

DEDICATION

To my children, grandchildren and the generations to come.

To Jenny Norton, Bob Ramsey and Bishop Jackie Green, three of God's spiritual giants.

To the people of this Nation who pray without ceasing to protect the integrity of the Nation; may your Godly endeavors be blessed as you pray for the United States of America.

To Dr. William S. Starr, whose prayers changed the trajectory of my life.

FOREWORD

Standing on the Wall: Prayers to Preserve the Integrity of a Nation was a result of sharing the Word of God and praying for the Nation. It is a prayer guide that shares well-known scriptures and applies the Word of God by praying them over America. This book and the scriptural context is specifically assembled for America's people and their unique role in joining together to pray for the integrity of the Nation.

My greatest desire - to activate, by the power of the Holy Spirit, the hearts of America's leaders and future leaders to, "protect the integrity of this Nation through prayer."

People are encouraged to reflect on the prayers in this book and think about how to pray for those who govern the Nation. As you spend quiet times in the morning and evening; *clothe* yourself in the Word of God and these simple prayers. Watch God work in and through you for His glory and for the preservation of America!

God tells us that the integrity of a nation will lead to guidance, while perversity will lead to destruction:

The integrity of the upright will guide them, But the perversity of the unfaithful will destroy them.
Proverbs 11:3

And because of this scripture, the integrity of our leaders must be the hallmark by which they lead:

Fear the LORD and judge with integrity, for the LORD our God does not tolerate perverted justice, partiality, or the taking of bribes.
2 Chronicles 9:17

America is a Nation blessed and highly favored by God, yet troubled with many afflictions. I sincerely believe that the Lord will deliver the Nation out of them all.

As we humble ourselves, pray, seek His face and turn from wicked ways – then, He promises to hear us, forgive us, and heal our land.

(2 Chronicles 7:14, paraphrased)

America has a *national constitution,* and we need our leaders to honor it. But there is also a **spiritual constitution,** that must be constantly developed in our leaders and its people to preserve our democracy.

America must be a Nation where its leaders are not on one side or another, but on the side of the Sovereign Creator!

As you reflect and pray, believe:

• America is a Nation of integrity, living under the commanded blessing of the Lord (united).

(Psalm 133)

• The integrity of America is a critical element in global affairs.

• America is presently under spiritual attack from various rulers, principalities and spiritual wickedness in high places, but this is not new.

• America has overcome significant scourges in the past, and

• God will deliver us out of them all again, if we humble ourselves, pray, seek His face and turn from wicked ways.

(2 Chronicles 7:14, paraphrased)

Jannah Scott

BEFORE YOU READ
THIS BOOK

This book is written for anyone who desires to see the Nation united under the guidance, protection, and banner of Our Lord Jesus Christ. This is not the politicized Jesus that has been spoken of so many times to point fingers, to promote political agendas and to keep the Nation divided.

This book is written in the spirit of Jesus who is a steadfast anchor for our Nation's Soul. The Jesus who said, "If I be lifted up, I will draw all people unto myself." (John 12:32) The Jesus who said, "Lord let them be one even as You and I are one." (John 17:22) The Jesus who said, "the greatest commandments are that we love God with all our heart, soul, mind and strength and we love our neighbors as we love ourselves."
(Mark 12:30-31, paraphrased)

This is the Jesus of whom the prophet Isaiah spoke when he said, "God will appoint salvation for walls and bulwarks. Open the gates that the righteous nation which keeps the truth may enter in. You will keep him in perfect peace whose mind is stayed on You because he trusts in You! Trust in the Lord forever, for in YAH (God), the Lord is Everlasting strength." (Isaiah 26:1-4)

So, no matter your own faith, tradition or preference, you are encouraged to read this book and reflect on how you can use these prayers to preserve the integrity of our Nation. Let these prayers guide you as you pray for our Nation.

If we all pray these prayers together, in unity, we as a Nation − like the mythological Phoenix − will rise out of the ashes of division, desperation and despair and achieve our divine destiny.

PRAYER FOR PEOPLE TO BE SAVED

This prayer is for those who have not yet accepted or come to know Jesus as their Lord and Savior, but who want to receive this book and who want to pray these prayers for our Nation.

Dear God, I thank You for the gracious gift that You've given the world through Your Son Jesus Christ; who was born of a virgin; who lived a life of the common man; who performed miracles, signs and wonders; who led many unto You for the Salvation of their soul; who went to the cross for our sins; who defeated death, hell and the grave; who rose again, is seated at Your right hand, full of grace and truth; and will come again to judge the living and the dead.

I ask that the person reading this book now, who may not know Jesus as Lord and Savior read the following prayer with me.

Jannah Scott

"Lord Jesus, I am a sinner, but by God's grace, You died for my sins. Please come into my heart, please make me brand new, please let me experience the joy of Your salvation as one who believes. Jesus, I live my life for You, that even as You wish, I wish that none would perish. I commit to sharing Your Lordship, Your Salvation, and Your goodness with others, so they would come to know that You are Lord and Savior of this great Nation and will have a *salvation* perspective, eternal perspective.

Thank You for coming into my heart, I receive You today as my Lord and Savior. God thank You for it is in Jesus' name that I pray, believing that You hear me and that You will answer according to Your will for the divine destiny of the United States of America to come forth. Amen."

TABLE OF CONTENTS

PART IV.
Prayers for the Nation

Special Issue Prayers

Transportation Systems Sector

Prayers of Faith

PART 1

THE UNITED STATES OF AMERICA:
BLESSED IS THE NATION WHOSE GOD IS THE LORD

The land on which your feet have walked will be your inheritance and that of your children forever because you have wholly followed the Lord my God. And now behold the Lord has kept me alive, as He Said, these forty-five years...

Joshua 14:9-10 (NIV)

God has preserved men and women in past times simply because of His Word. Therefore, it is important for people to pray God's Word over this Nation, that it might be preserved for us and for our posterity. The number forty-five means preservation. It is not a coincidence then, that during the 45th presidency, we have been led to pray for the preservation of the Nation, particularly its integrity.

A GAPING HOLE

Over the past several decades, a gaping hole has been worn in the consciousness of America. Not only do we suffer debilitating financial debt, that, if not paid, could forfeit the future of our children's children for generations to come. But there is also a *spiritual debt* that has been amassed, by the manifestation of the seven deadly sins:

- Pride
- Greed (Avarice)
- Lust
- Envy
- Gluttony
- Wrath
- Sloth

This spiritual debt, just like the financial debt, must be paid for America to survive, thrive and fulfill its original intent.

THE CONSTITUTION: OUR FOUNDING PRINCIPLES FOR PRESERVATION

We are told America was founded on Christian principles, right? Whether you agree or not, it is clear that God has set this Nation high upon a hill as a light to many other nations. The principles which are found in the preamble of the US Constitution seek to provide for the integrity of the Nation based on principles that were first presented in the Holy Bible:

We the People of the United States, in Order to form a more perfect **Union** (John 17, Psalm 133:1, 3b), establish **Justice** (Micah 6:8, Amos 5:24), insure domestic **Tranquility** (Philippians 4:7, Romans 12:18), provide for the **Common Defense** (Nehemiah 4:14, 17-18, Numbers 31:3, Psalm 46:1), promote the **General Welfare** (Deuteronomy

15:7-11, Romans 15:1-2) and secure the **Blessings of Liberty** (Luke 4:18, Deuteronomy 28:1-14) to ourselves and our **Posterity** (Psalm 102:18-28, Psalm 22:30-31), do ordain and establish this Constitution for the United States of America.

But are we living these principles today?

Unity: Do our interactions form a more perfect union, or do we violate our own Constitution with our divisiveness?

Justice: Do we establish Godly justice or do we oppress the poor, yet pardon the rich and call that justice?

Tranquility: Do we ensure peace, both personal and public, or is chaos and confusion the order of the day?

Common Defense: Do we rightfully identify our enemies and provide for the common defense, or do we simply seek to defend ourselves against those with whom we do not agree?

General Welfare: Do we use the power of taxation to promote general public welfare, or to satisfy the desires of highly lobbied special interests?

Blessings of Liberty: Do our actions in all branches of government secure the blessings of liberty? Or is freedom just available to those who can afford to pay?

Posterity (Generations): Do we hold our actions up to the light of what they mean for future generations? Or do we just do what feels and sounds good for now?

I have lived a long time, Sir, a long time, and the longer I live, the more convincing proofs I see of this truth— that God governs in the affairs of men. And if a sparrow cannot fall to the ground without his notice, is it probable that an empire can rise without his aid?

Benjamin Franklin
Constitutional Convention, 1787

23

THE DECLARATION
OF INDEPENDENCE:
A SACRED HONOR

...And for the support of this Declaration, with a firm reliance on the protection of divine Providence, we mutually pledge to each other our Lives, our Fortunes and our Sacred Honor.

Have we discarded the sacred covenant of our constitution and our declaration with one another? How do we regain the original intent of our Founders' sense of loyalty, brotherhood, compassion and care, and a sacred honoring of one another?

If we continue to remove the Word of God from the foundation of our government, we run the risk of fundamental collapse. The basic fabric (ideals) of this Nation is woven with the Word of God.

The Bible is the foundation of our political constitution. It must also be re-established as the foundation of this Nation's spiritual constitution. This can only be done when America's leaders and its people begin to call on the divine providence of God to intervene in the affairs of men.

PRAYER TO PRESERVE AMERICA

"Preserve America, oh God, let her take refuge in You. Let America trust in the Almighty! LORD we ask You to preserve the integrity of America and keep us alive; let this Nation be blessed upon the earth. Father, please show America the path of life: Let her people seek after Your presence, for in Your presence is fullness of joy; at Your right hand there are pleasures forevermore.

Almighty God, we come humbly before you on bended knee, beseeching You on behalf of this great Nation, America. You have set this Nation on high in the earth, and for that we are forever grateful. You have a divine destiny for America, oh God, that can only be achieved as we keep our hearts and minds fixed on You.

So we cry out today, oh God, for You to do what only You can – cause us to remember who we are and Whose we are! Restore to us the joy of our salvation! Let us come as a Nation to You in repentance, awe and reverence. Let our cries for forgiveness lay a path for America's preservation.

God, bless and keep America, sustain America, let Your Holy Angels guard America! Lord make Your face shine upon America; be gracious to America! Lift up Your face toward America, and give her peace, tranquility and a way of life that is acceptable to You."

(Adapted from Psalm 16:1, 11; Psalm 41:2 and Numbers 6:24-26, AMP)

PART 2

STANDING ON THE WALL FOR THE INTEGRITY OF A NATION

INTEGRITY DEFINED

What does this mean, integrity of a Nation? Technically, it means the state of being whole and undivided: or as *Merriam-Webster Dictionary* states – a state of unity; coherence; cohesion; solidarity; togetherness. It can also mean adherence to moral and ethical principles; soundness of moral character and honesty.

The word in the Hebrew (*tom*- H8537 in Strong's Concordance) comes from the root *tamam* (H8552) which translates to "accomplished, perfect, finished, done." When this Nation was founded, it was intended to be a work of integrity, a finished work, a perfect union, done.

Men and women have stood up and fought for the principles of integrity – upon which this Nation was founded.

INTEGRITY OF A NATION:
UNDER ATTACK

Today, we are in a fight, but thank
God the weapons of our warfare need
not be carnal – biting words, heaved
insults, slander or worse. Our most
effective weapons will be those that
are *mighty in God for the pulling down
of strongholds, casting down arguments,
and every high thing that would exalt
itself against the knowledge of God...*
(2 Corinthians 10:3-5)

When did we stop listening fully
to each other? The prophet Isaiah
reminds us to come and reason
together...   (Isaiah 1:18)

INTEGRITY OF A NATION:
PRESERVED

We must decree the restoration of
civility with one another. How do we
reclaim civility in our society?

We call out and claim victory over

the perilous times as described in 2 Timothy 3:

...men will be lovers of themselves, lovers of money, boasters, proud, blasphemers, disobedient to parents, unthankful, unholy, unloving, unforgiving, slanderers, without self-control, brutal, despisers of good, traitors, headstrong, haughty, lovers of pleasure rather than lovers of God, having a form of godliness but denying its power.

In this 45th term of presidency, we believe that leaders and people acting together, under the divine guidance of God, can stem the tide of these perilous times. By doing so, God will restore this Nation to its original principled intent and preserve its integrity.

INTEGRITY OF A NATION: CHARACTER

Loving Father, faithful God! Thank You for giving Your people a sense of what it means to be a person of character. Let the leaders of this Nation seek to emulate the character of Jesus (Philippians 2:5). Let the Nation see leaders not curse or be condescending toward one another.

Our Nation needs leaders with strength of character – men and women who express dignity, honesty, purity of speech, holiness, righteousness and truth (Colossians 3:12). Give our leaders character that is rooted in the Fruit of the Spirit! Give them character that exudes love, joy, peace, endurance, gentleness, kindness, meekness, faith and self-control (Galatians 5:22-23). Such character shall give our leaders and the Nation hope in You, and You never disappoint (Romans 5:3-5).

We *call out* unnecessary foul language and actions, where the hearts and minds of Your children could be polluted by leadership that is not honoring You.

We *call forth* dignity in how our leaders carry themselves, focused on the higher things of God.

(Colossians 3:2)

We commit to resolve our differences in civil language and tone, not seeking to subdue the other's opinion with harsh, defiling words.

(Colossians 4:6)

We pray for our leaders to approach governance with a heart of humility, not thinking more highly of themselves or the positions they hold.

(Romans 12:3)

God, give Your leaders the mind, wisdom and temperament of Christ, whose anger only arose when the people dishonored You (John 2:12-17). Let the character of this Nation's leaders be ever honoring to You, O Sovereign God! In Jesus' name. Amen.

PART 3

THE CALL TO STAND: ATTENTION, AMERICA!

HOW WE STAND

Regardless of what we see in the natural, God calls His leaders and His people to *see* (discern, get wisdom, knowledge and understanding) in the Spirit. No matter what we see, God calls His leaders and His people to stand in the full armor of God.

(Ephesian 6; 1 Timothy 2:1-3)

We must stand in faith with God. We must stand in the power and might of God. We must stand and speak forth what God tells us to say until our voices are heard. We must stand when all seems lost and there is nothing else to do or say.

WHEN WE STAND

We must stand in the midst of the terrors and the disappointments of our days. We must stand against injustice and unrighteousness that seeks to cover the land.

WHY WE STAND

Everyone who calls on the name of the Lord is supposed to stand. Let us not be among those who God could not find in the day of indignation. God is looking for one to stand in the gap on behalf of the land, so He does not utterly destroy it!

(Ezekiel 3:22, paraphrased)

WILL WE STAND?

We're asking God to heal the land in this day, but are we willing to stand? Are we willing to humble ourselves, pray, turn from our wicked ways so that God will hear from heaven, forgive our sins and heal our land?

We must stand and pray for the peace of the place where God has led us. Of all the acreage on the planet where we could live, we live in the United States of America. Because the words of leaders of the free world can shift the trajectory of the planet, our leaders must be people of prayer.

So, together, we must stand at the gates of America, and in the paraphrased words of the Prophet Jeremiah:

Seek the peace and prosperity of America and pray to the Lord for it like never before! For in its peace we will have peace.

Jeremiah 29:7 (paraphrased)

PART 4

PRAYERS FOR THE NATION

PRESERVATION

Each year, national government officials examine the *current and future* state of the Nation to determine where America is strongest, where the Nation may be at risk, and where precious resources must be applied. This concept also applies to the *spiritual state* and future of the Nation; and by wisdom, knowledge and understanding we can discern where the Nation is strong, where it is at risk, and where to appropriately apply the spiritual resources of intercession.

Arise, Oh America! Shine, for your light has come, and the glory of the Lord rises upon you. See, darkness covers the earth and thick darkness is over the peoples, but the Lord rises upon you

and his glory appears over you.
(Isaiah 60:1-2, paraphrased)

I have posted watchmen on your walls, America; they will never be silent day or night. You who call on the Lord, give yourselves no rest, and give Him no rest till He establishes America and makes her the praise of the earth.

Pass through, pass through the gates! Prepare the way for the people. Build up, build up the highway! Remove the stones. Raise a banner for the nations. The Lord has made proclamation to the ends of the earth: "...They will be called the Holy People, the Redeemed of the Lord; and you will be called Sought After, the City No Longer Deserted."
(Isaiah 62:6-7, 10-12, NIV)

God, we thank You for the preservation of America, for its integrity as a Nation and as a people. We thank You that the attack against this Nation in the 1800's was

thwarted by the humble prayers and spoken words of one of America's greatest presidents, Abraham Lincoln. Through his second inaugural address, You showed us that the humble thoughts and prayers of one man in the highest position of national authority could stop the destruction of this Nation and its people:

"Shall we discern therein any departure from those divine attributes which the believers in a Living God always ascribe to Him? Fondly do we hope, fervently do we pray, that this mighty scourge of war may speedily pass away. Yet, if God wills that it continue until all the wealth piled by the bondman's two-hundred and fifty years of unrequited toil shall be sunk, and until every drop of blood drawn with the lash, shall be paid by another drawn with the sword, as was said three thousand years ago, so still it must be said, the judgments of the Lord, are true and righteous altogether.

With malice toward none; with charity for all; with firmness in the right, as God gives us to see the right, let us strive on to finish the work we are in; to bind up the Nation's wounds; to care for him who shall have borne the battle, and for his widow, and his orphan, to do all which may achieve and cherish a just, and a lasting peace, among ourselves, and with all nations."

Second Inaugural Address
March 4, 1865

Although he was assassinated for his stance, God, we know that You honored President Abraham Lincoln and his posterity. We see this in the national remembrances and significant shifts in the fabric of a society that was headed for destruction.

We thank You God, that You are raising up other presidents with this same heart to preserve the integrity of America. And we pray for those presidents even now, that You would make Yourself ever present in the lives of all presidents, current and future. Let the words that flow from their mouths be pleasing and acceptable in Your sight.

FOR THE NATION AS A WHOLE

As the heaven is high above this Nation, so let Your mercy be upon us. From everlasting to everlasting, You are God. Have compassion upon this Nation, Lord and send us Your mercy. Break up the fallow ground of our Nation's heart so that the TRUTH OF GOD is preserved.

As we pray for the Nation and all who dwell therein, we pray for open minds focused on the mind of Christ. Let our prayers affect movement in the heavenly realms on behalf of a Nation in crisis.

Give us the discernment to pray, decree and declare those things that You care about; not just today, not just for the present time. Let our prayers for this Nation have a positive impact for generations to come. God, we pray for this Nation to reconnect with You and lift Your name above the governing authorities — turn this Nation back to the True, Holy and Sovereign God!

Thank You God, for making every crooked path straight and breaking up fallow ground, so that things we must address as a people can be revealed.

Thank You for placing a special anointing on this Nation to use wisdom to move forward in Your will.

Thank You that the heart of this Nation is sober and consecrated to You, as we think and pray about all that must come to pass.

Thank You, Lord, that as a Nation, the rights You have already given us and the sanctity of its original intent shall be preserved.

Thank and praise You God, for You have raised up (and are continuing to raise up) more men and women of integrity who can go into leadership positions. Keep this country on the path of Your original intent.

Let us grow wiser and stronger in Your Word, not weaker.

Let us grow more respectful and insightful of Your Word, not irreverent.

Let us grow more in the way of holiness and consecration, not in the way of Sodom and Gomorrah. We thank and praise You for Your promises, in Jesus' name. Amen.

CIVILITY

Oh, that we would speak with one another in Psalms and hymns and spiritual songs! Oh, that the sounds of our voices would rest upon the ears of the hearer like the dew in the morning. Oh, that our words would be like salt gently seasoning the conversations of our day. Oh, that the rivers flowing from our mouths would be like *Rivers of Life* encouraging, empowering, and enlightening one another.

Heavenly Father, You have given us brains to think, emotions upon which to act and mouths to speak. As I come to You today, I pray for thoughts, speech and actions that are tempered

by the power of the Holy Spirit. Please show Your people a renewed way of communicating with one another that is in accordance with Your Word. Let not our thoughts stray from that which, according to Philippians 4:7-8, is good, kind, holy, of good report. Let not our words defile, desecrate or demean the very presence of the Holy Spirit within each person. Rather, *speaking the truth in love, we are to grow up in every way into Him who is the head, into Christ.*
Ephesians 4:15 (ESV)

Let not our actions align with the powers of darkness but instead bring light and life to every situation we encounter.

Father we also pray for greater understanding for those who have been uncivil. Let them understand that such thoughts, words and actions are destructive to their own eternity and to future generations.

...on the day of judgment people will give account for every careless word they speak, for by your words you will be justified, and by your words you will be condemned.

Matthew 12:36-37 (ESV)

Death and life are in the power of the tongue and those that love it shall eat the fruit thereof.

Proverbs 18:21 (KJV)

They profess to know God, but they deny Him by their works and their words. They are detestable, disobedient, unfit for any good work. We take authority over the root spirits of lack of civility and we command hatred, division, pride, greed, and unchecked hostility to go in Jesus' name.

Hatred: We cast out hate and speak unconditional love over the human family, in Jesus' name.

Division: We speak unity and the commanded blessing that comes with it, over our families, communities, Nation and the nations of the world in Jesus' name.

Pride: We pull down the principality of pride over people and groups, the pride which says, "I must be right at all times and at all costs" – we say pride must go in Jesus' name.

Greed: We take authority over the spirit of greed which results in lack of civility because the *spirit of me, myself and I* that wants everything and wants others to have nothing. We declare that there is more than enough in Jesus for all!

Ignorance of the Other: We take authority over the spirit of ignorance of the *other*, which breeds fear. We say that America's people will gain a supernatural ability to see the divine in others. Through this ability to see, they will begin to know and love one another.

Unchecked Hostility: We come against unchecked hostility and we decree in the courts of heaven that such a wicked, selfish spirit is bound, fettered and chained in Jesus' name.

We loose the spirit of agreement and reason over the people of America in the name of Jesus.

RECONCILIATION

We call for the spirit of reconciliation to arise. We loose the spirit of reconciliation in the name of Jesus as His ambassadors.
(2 Corinthians 5:18-20)

We bind relational fragmentation and confrontation and we loose peace, harmony and unity in Jesus' name!

We declare that the people of this Nation will be kind and compassionate to one another, forgiving each other as Christ has forgiven us.
(Ephesians 4:32, paraphrased, NIV)

Mighty God, I pray for those who profess to follow You, yet have not come to know the way of forgiveness and reconciliation.

I pray, even as the words of Jesus spoke, that where we have differences with others in the faith, instead of questioning their faith, we would leave our offerings at the altar. First go and be reconciled to them, then we will come back and offer our gifts to You, oh Lord.

Surely as You create America anew, old ways, things and habits must pass away and yes, all things must become new.

(Matthew 5:24,
2 Corinthians 9:18-21)

As we become new, the Nation puts on the mantle of *ambassadors of reconciliation*. Our leaders must first reconcile one with another, and then manifest the great promise of American leaders as reconciling ambassadors to nations of the world!

We believe for this promise with all our hearts and we commit this prayer to You this day!

CULTURE OF PEACE & HARMONY

Oh, Wonderful Counselor, Almighty God, Everlasting Father, Prince of Peace! We are promised that the government would be upon His shoulder and that His Kingdom of Peace shall never end.

We pray for the peace and prosperity of the Nation and its people. Not a false peace where people do not have a sense of who You are, but a peace that surpasses all understanding, such peace as only You, the Author of Peace, can bring us God.

While there must be wars, rumors of wars, pestilence, and earthquakes in diverse places, let us understand that these signs are only the beginning of birth pains.

The whole Nation writhes in pain, from one crisis to another. Just like a mother in labor, if we breathe in the breath of God, in every apparent painful contraction, we will be able to make it through the height of disharmony.

Even more so, give us spiritual strategies like the midwife, who helps the mother in labor sense the pain coming, and helps her strategize how to *mitigate*, even *eliminate* the pain.

God, we pray for a *culture of peace* to encapsulate the life of this Nation and its people. That we would even begin to greet each other with greetings of peace (Shalom). Let *peace* be more than just a word. Let it represent the thoughts we think, the words we speak, the actions we take. We believe that this is Your plan for America, Your thoughts toward America.

We pray that peace would begin at conception, that mothers' wombs would be a place of peace for the generations they carry.

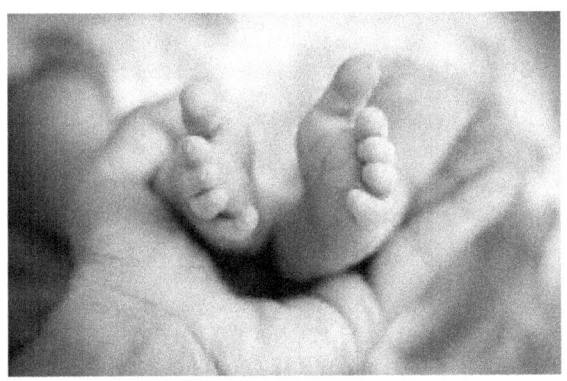

We pray that the truth about abortion – as the destruction of human life – will be revealed in the hearts of America's leaders. As the Lord says Let America *Choose Life*.
   (Deuteronomy 30:15, paraphrased)

We pray that domestic and random violence against pregnant women would cease. We pray for peace of the littlest Americans, whose best development – neurological, physical, spiritual, mental – depends on an environment of peace.

God, we pray for peace among the school children! We ask that their learning environment and the place they live, which shapes them for future adulthood would prioritize the practice, teaching and impartation of a spirit of PEACE!

Let there be peace, Heavenly Father, in the hearts and minds of our young adults, many who are are searching for meaning. Let them find meaning and purpose in their choices. Let those decisions guide them into a peaceful mindset.

We pray peace for those who are entering the prime of life. Let not a spirit of ungodly competition come upon them to achieve only material gain and worldly acclaim. But let their hearts and minds come to know the peace that only You can bring.

We speak peace over the elders of this Nation, who have built America to the position of greatness that it has become today. We pray that they know they are not forgotten, that the *old ways* have not been disregarded. Let them know that the foundation that they built, although in areas must be replaced, is being strengthened and expanded upon for even greater things in the generations to come.

We ask that You bring peace to still the trouble in our Nation. Allow hope in Christ (the anointing; the presence of God) to blanket this land; for in Him, the Prince of Peace, we have a blessed assurance of peace. In Jesus' name. Amen.

GOD-ORDAINED DISTRIBUTION OF WEALTH & PROSPERITY

Most Holy and Kind God, the earth is Yours and the fullness thereof; the world and they that dwell therein.

(Psalm 24:1, KJV)

You own the cattle on a thousand hills.

(Psalm 50:10, NIV)

And You are well-able to do exceedingly abundantly more than we could ever ask or think.

(Ephesians 3:20)

Help our national leaders to operate and lead this Nation like they have an understanding of who You are! You are God of Abundance! Wealth and riches belong to You.

This is why we come to You in prayer
for the God-ordained distribution
of wealth and prosperity in America.
Lord as we think about the disparity
between rich and poor in our Nation,
our hearts are grieved, and our spirits
shaken.

• While the net worth of wealth for
  most Americans has fallen, that of
  a small number of the wealthiest in
  the Nation has risen.

• Wealth disparities among races
  has widened to as much as 13:1.

God, some would say, even Jesus said, "the poor we will always have with us." (Matthew 26:11, paraphrased) But we ask, "How can this be?"

So we cry out for those who are suffering in abject poverty in a land of abundance:

- We cry out for children who go to sleep without a meal or a decent place to lay their heads.

- We cry out for frail, forgotten elders – who have given their lives for the benefit of others – who live in squalor, eating food meant for animals.

- We cry out for people who suffer and die from treatable illnesses because of the lack of money to get the proper treatment.

God, how can we understand the impact of such inequality on unfairly oppressed people as God's divine will?

So, we come on bended knee, asking for wisdom, knowledge and understanding as to how wealth can be properly and divinely distributed in this Nation. In a market economy, we need Your divine wisdom of how to balance equity and regulation, how to close the gap between rich and poor, how to serve You, oh God of all creation, and not mammon.

• We pray for Your divine guidance to understand, so that the right decisions for the good of all Americans can be made.

• We pray for wisdom, relative to the tax code of this Nation, to shut the door on unfair practices that allow some with so much wealth to avoid contributing to the needs of the country.

• We pray for the spirit of divine wealth distribution, according to Acts 4:31-37, to come upon this Nation, so that the basic needs of every American is met.

• We pray against the spirit of gluttony, greed and the glorification of riches in the social consciousness of our society. We declare that those with ridiculous amounts of wealth will begin to give freely to build up the old waste places. We say those with imbalanced amounts of wealth will begin to, according to Isaiah chapter 58, restore the breaches in our land and repair the streets of our cities, towns and communities so that all can live.

Lord, we pray for the design and implementation of laws that would stop unfair economic practices, unjust investments and oppressive barriers to economic justice for all. God, we ask for wisdom, guidance and motivation for wealthy Americans to return to a simple, basic lifestyle – without excess – so that others may simply live.

We pray on behalf of the divine distribution of wealth among future generations, and we say that we shall leave an inheritance to our children's children. In Jesus' name we pray. Amen.

(Proverbs 13:22)

FOR THE MIND OF CHRIST TO WIPE OUT THE SCOURGE OF ISMs INTENSE SMALL MINDEDNESS

Let this mind be in you which was also in Christ Jesus.
Philippians 2:5

These words from the Apostle Paul begin our prayer for a mind that is humble, obedient to Your ways oh God!

We will not be conformed to the various *isms* of this world, but we are praying that we can be transformed by the renewing of our minds.

Not thinking more highly of ourselves than we should, we ask for a mind that focuses on how we can best serve Your will in the earth, dear Lord.

(Romans 12:1-3, paraphrased)

We pray for God-ordained leaders of this Nation to strive against every *ism* that would rear its ugly head and seek to limit the hearts and minds of the people of America.

We pray that America's leaders will promote the establishment of decrees, laws, resolutions, judgments and even executive orders and policies to deny the spirit of small-mindedness to take hold.

We come against all forms of bigotry, racism and ethnic division.

We come against the ideology of life without God (humanism), and *isms* deceptively disguised as religious freedom.

We deny classism; caste systems and *isms* that would perpetuate a system of haves and have nots.

We will not stand for *isms* and actions that would turn genders against each other for the sake of personal, political or monetary gain.

We will not stand for people with different abilities to be ridiculed, marginalized or set aside in society.

We will not allow the things we do not understand to be a justification for fear, oppression, ostracism, hatred and maltreatment of others.

We declare the words of the Apostle Peter, that when it comes to what really matters, the eternal salvation of our soul, we are all the same in Christ our Lord.

(Galatians 3:26-28, paraphrased)

Thank You Mighty God for the people who You place in the Office of President. Let the President be consecrated unto You. Let the President be sold out only to God, not to special interests, not to ungodly alliances.

Let the President act upon Your Word and allow the President to accomplish those things necessary so that America may be healed. Lord,

we pray that you cover the President so that this global leader will not be swayed to the right or the left, but be preserved.

We pray for the President to come under Your divine, solemn influence. Keep the President's foot from slipping and allow his decisions to be guided by You alone.

We declare good health to the President so that the responsibilities of the office will not cause undue sickness or premature death. We say that the President is of a sound mind and operates in the power of God and in love. May uprightness and integrity guide the President, so that he will fix his gaze directly on You, oh Lord. He will give careful thought to the path his feet take. He will be steadfast, keeping his feet from evil.

We pray that You would make Yourself ever present in the President's life. Let the words that flow from the President's mouth be words that are pleasing and acceptable in Your sight, and let not evil advisors whisper evil thoughts and actions in the President's ear.

God let this Nation and world be enlightened by the words and actions of this President, and use this President to turn America back to You, oh Holy One.

We ask for forgiveness for those who have dishonored the sacred mantle over the office by ignorantly dishonoring the person occupying it.

We pray for wisdom as to what the office represents. When there is disagreement, we pray for understanding and for a civil way to find solutions.

We pray for repentance and a turnaround of uncivil behavior among leadership. Let a spirit of conviction come upon those who must repent so that the Nation shall be healed.

Mighty God, we ask that You guide the President, and let not our enemies' triumph over us! Integrity is a watch word for the leader of the free world; You uphold America and keep her in Your presence forever!

(Psalm 41:11)

KINGDOM CAUCUS IN THE UNITED STATES CONGRESS

We praise You, oh God for the revelation of a *Kingdom Caucus in the US Congress.* This Kingdom Caucus is made up of people who will not focus on partisan politics, positions, posturing or power.

They will instead form a Kingdom Caucus for the glory of God in government. This Kingdom Caucus shall legislate according to the will of God! This Kingdom Caucus will pray like Solomon who prayed for wisdom as to how to govern the people! This Kingdom Caucus will stand against the principalities and powers that seek to infiltrate American society through unjust laws, policies and behind-closed-door deals.

This Kingdom Caucus will stand for God in the public square, gather the people and pray like Samuel did to rebuild the soul of the Nation. This Kingdom Caucus will stand as God's agents in government and rededicate this Nation, its leaders, its people and its progeny to You, oh God, in Jesus' name!

We decree a coming forth of this Kingdom Caucus now in Jesus' name, and we declare that every ungodly congressional caucus becomes a rotten carcass, a stench in the nostrils of the Lord!

Thank You oh God, for extricating every rotten carcass from the hallowed halls of Congress. Let Your Kingdom Caucus draw Your leaders to a Godly form of governance, in Jesus' name. Amen!

Inspired by Prophet
Cathy Fontenot

ALL ELECTED & APPOINTED OFFICIALS

Thank You Mighty God, that as in the days of Jehoshaphat, Your leaders take delight in You. Thank You that even as they make laws based on man's system, they will meditate on Your law, Your Word, which makes man to prosper.

Let them meditate on Your Holy Word and share the divine principles upon which this Nation was founded. And let them share it in practical ways as they lead, so that the glory of the Mighty God will fall on all the people, even as in the days of Jehoshaphat.

God, we pray against ungodly alliances. We pray

that our leaders will not be swayed
by gifts and cunning speech to make
partnerships and deals with wicked
rulers and self-centered people.

God, we pray for great discernment
and strength for our leaders to
withstand every temptation. Please
allow our leaders to look to You, oh
God, for help in making righteous
decisions.

Lord, You know the countenance of
Your leaders. Men and women who
have committed their lives in public
service to You.

We are not unaware of the cunning
attacks, perverted plans and demonic
forces that would seek to use human
frailties to derail the destiny of God
for this Nation.

We pray that every occultic, evil spirit
that would try to persuade our leaders
to turn to evil acts would be bound.

Let their spirit, soul, mind and body line up with the truth and will of God.

We ask You God, to endow Your leaders, with a spirit to trust You with all their hearts. Put a fire in their bellies for Your will, oh God, to be done.

Let not mercy and truth forsake them, but let them bind Your commandments and Your truth about their necks and write them upon the tables of their hearts.

(Proverbs 7:3, paraphrased, KJV)

Thank You, God, for raising up Your prophets who will not just tell leaders what they want to hear. But like Micaiah, they will speak what God says, no matter the cost.

We thank You, Lord, that our national leaders will not be led astray or deceived by lying prophets, prognosticators or those trying to manipulate the people for profit, regardless of political persuasion.

We thank You for the order of the Lord that comes upon the branches of government – the White House (Executive Branch), Congress (Legislative Branch), the Supreme Court (along with its district courts, Judicial Branch). We say that every lying spirit, every false prognosticator and those who would seek to profit from chaos and confusion in this Nation must flee, in Jesus' name!

Let our national leaders, hear and harken to Your voice, oh God, to bring forth healing in this Nation. Let them seek to keep the unity in the bond of peace. We believe that even as in the time of Jehoshaphat, there are leaders in these houses of government who will bow their heads and fall on their faces before You. We believe that they will worship alone or collectively and cry out to You, so that the entire Nation shall be blessed.

God, we know You can work through these leaders. But what is it that we must do so that Your mighty hand of justice, mercy, compassion and Your promise of greatness will be on this Nation?

We pray for the hearts of our leaders to be loyal to You and to Your Word. You are looking for those who are loyal to You so that You can show Yourself strong in America!

We take authority over those things that try to distract their loyalties away from God – even those things that seem good, but are not of God. Protect them, we pray from those thoughts in their own minds that may be good, but are not God's ordained best for the people.

From generation to generation, You have shown Yourself strong to those who are loyal to You. Let this not be the generation that becomes disloyal to the Sovereign God! Let them not forget Your promises spoken over this Nation through the mouths of the founding fathers from centuries past: that America would be a light to other nations; that freedom would ring throughout the land; that all men are created equal; and that all would have the inalienable rights of life, liberty and the pursuit of happiness.

PEOPLE OF AMERICA SPECIAL CONSIDERATION FOR RURAL AND INNER CITIES

Mighty God we pray for the people of America! We pray for those in the cities and those in the fields (rural areas). Mighty God we pray first and foremost that the people of America will turn back to You. We acknowledge the sins of the Nation and the iniquities of the people who have been ever before You.

We ask, oh God, for a cleansing fire to come upon the people of this Nation – a fire that burns away everything that is not of You. Send a purifying fire that removes the dross; a fire that will burn in our hearts so that we turn in repentance and yearn again, for intimacy with the One True God!

Forgive us our sins, oh God, as we have sinned against You and each other. Remove the separation that hangs between us and You, and bring us unto Your bosom again, oh God! Father, let us not be so concerned about the things of life, what we shall eat, drink or wear. Let us not focus on who we are aligned with politically or with whom we agree or disagree. We will not be concerned with who looks like, worships like, talks like, dresses like or thinks like us! But let us seek first Your kingdom and its righteousness, and all these other things be added according to Your will.

Lord God we need a fresh infilling of Your Holy Spirit! Let the *ruach* (Holy Spirit) breath of God blow through the empty places of our lives.

For those who will receive You, we are grateful for Your love and everlasting mercy; but for those who will not receive You, even after all the warnings, we say Lord have Your way! For surely the Word of the Lord shall come to pass in that day, that every knee shall bow, every tongue shall confess that You are Lord, to the glory of the Father and of His Son, Our Savior, Jesus. AMEN.

Oh, King of Glory, Lord, strong and mighty over this Nation, we ask You to set the captives free and bring liberty to the people of America!

Heavenly Father, we praise You for the people of America, who are called by Your name. Let us continue to humble ourselves like never before, let us continue to pray for this Nation, seek Your face and turn from wickedness. Then we await Your promise to hear us, forgive our sins and heal our land.

Blessed shall the people of America be in the city, blessed shall they be in the field. Then all the peoples of the earth shall see that the people of America are called by Your name and they shall fear us because of our God!

You promise to open to us Your good treasure, the heavens, to give the rain to this land in due season and to bless the work of our hands. And we shall not turn aside from any of the words You have commanded us, to the right or to the left, to go after other gods to serve them — especially the god of mammon. We ask for these blessings to come upon the people of America who are called by Your name, oh Lord! In Jesus' name.

TRIBAL NATIONS ON WHOSE NATIVE LAND WE STAND

Dear God, we bow our heads in appreciation of the federally and state recognized Tribal Nations.

Father, first and foremost, we repent for the savage brutality meted out upon our Native American brothers and sisters. These Native people have loved this land – Mother Earth – and sought to maintain its pristine nature for countless years. We repent as a Nation for the dishonorable practices:

- Slaughter of Indigenous Resources
- Indoctrination of Innocent Children
- Dishonored Treaties
- Abuse
- Hurtful Stereotypes
- Disease
- Separation of Families
- Destructive Elements
- Desecration of Holy Land
- Annihilation of a People

God please forgive us and our forefathers for wrongs done to our Native American neighbors. We rend our clothes and weep with tears for the deep hurts and destructive practices placed on them, even as they sought to embrace and assist the *other (non-First Nation humankind)*! Please forgive us, oh God! How we repent for seeking to *clothe* these despicable practices of our forefathers as Christian evangelism!

Forgive us, oh God, for misrepresenting the LOVE that is in Jesus.

We ask for a fresh wind of Your Holy Spirit to mend the relationship between Native Americans and *others*. Let repentance and efforts toward reconciliation come forth – among the people, among the states whose land adjoins Tribal Nations, and among the national leaders whose laws and policies impact the Tribal Nations. We pray for *hearts of clay* to manifest in the lives of those in authority so that this Nation will no longer ravage, pillage and abuse our Native American neighbors or their lands.

We pray for the Tribal Nations' people to be open to the true spirit of Jesus – the very presence of God and newness of life that was stolen from them through heinous acts of deception, depravation, destruction and death.

God, we pray for a turnaround in the generational destructive practices introduced into the lives of Native American people by colonizers.

We pray that others will appreciate the ancient knowledge of honoring and stewarding the earth that our indigenous brothers and sisters can teach us.

Let us allow ourselves to learn and incorporate their practices into our own patterns of earthly stewardship. We come against generational, genetically predisposed illness, such as fetal alcohol syndrome, alcoholism, diabetes, depression and other conditions that arose from the introduction of destructive practices by others. We loose divine health and access to health care for our Native American brothers and sisters, not just the treatment of disease, but the promotion of health, in Jesus' name!

We bind limited economies on the Tribal Nations! God, thank You that these economies will not be primarily dependent on casinos, but that You will give access, wisdom, knowledge and understanding to the hearts and minds of Tribal leaders for diversified economies – economies where their posterity can live, learn and grow without limits. We bind corrupt practices that would seek to continue to drain resources from the Tribal Nations! We loose greater knowledge of divine stewardship over all their assets, even as they steward the land, we pray. Cast out the devourer from among them, in Jesus' name!

We pray that Native Americans are being restored to their rightful places as people of great knowledge, skills and abilities of this earth and its rightful stewardship.

Lord, we thank You that these Nations, whether recognized by man or not, are recognized by You. You sent Your Son, Jesus, to bring liberty to Native Americans, as You did for us all. We pray for them to walk in liberty in the land which You gave them. We pray for the lives of future generations of Native Americans, that they may live long and prosper in this land. Amen.

US TERRITORIES AMERICAN SAMOA, GUAM, NORTHERN MARIANA ISLANDS, MIDWAY ISLANDS, PUERTO RICO, US VIRGIN ISLANDS

Almighty God we thank You for the US territories, lands and people groups who were once independent in their own right, but who through circumstances are now attached to the United States. These territories are located in areas where many natural disasters have hit and destroyed lands, livelihoods and futures.

We pray for the inhabitants in these territories, God, that first and foremost, freedom in Christ would be abundant and true for them. Secondly, that the promises of God would be made manifest in a greater way in the days to come. Promises of abundance, peace, safety and provisions. Promises for restoration and recovery from damages due to natural and man-made incidents.

We pray for the territories in the Pacific Ocean. Mighty God, please forgive us as a Nation for exploiting the beauty, resources and people of these islands. Give us wisdom, oh God, as to how we can humble ourselves to understand what they have to offer us in their traditions, their ways of living.

God forgive us for how we have been so wasteful and have lacked diligence in our use of Midway Island. Our daily conveniences (and the use and disposal of plastics) have damaged the islands' ecosystem. Forgive us, when we refused to acknowledge that our bad actions have an equally bad outcome for people and places thousands of miles away.

We pray for the territories in the Atlantic Ocean. Mighty God forgive us that while our forefathers took of these lands, we sometimes forget to acknowledge that they are now part of the US.

A spirit of ignorance would question the citizenship of people born in these places. Such ignorance would question their legitimacy to benefit from the abundance in the US that oftentimes would come from their lands.

Please forgive us for turning our back on the people of these territories. Please forgive us when we have looked down on them as second-class citizens.

Please forgive us Lord when we have used their lands for our own selfish pleasures. When they have had need, we have squabbled over whether or not we would help them.

Protect the people, the economies and the resources of these territories. We ask that You protect them from corrupt leaders. We ask that You allow them to know the joy and prosperity that only You can bring. Please allow

their children and the generations
to come to enjoy life, liberty and the
pursuit of happiness as Americans. In
Jesus' name. Amen.

PRESENT & FUTURE GENERATIONS

You oh Lord, rule forever! Your throne is from generation to generation. We acknowledge the greatness of Your signs, and the mighty wonder of Your works. Your kingdom is from everlasting to everlasting and Your dominion is from generation to generation!

We pray for America now, and we say that this is the generation of those who seek You, oh God, who seek Your face. We say this is the generation that will come to know You, even the children yet to be born.

This Nation shall arise and tell of who You are and of Your wondrous works to their children's children! This generation shall HEAR THE WORD OF THE LORD!

Even as the Apostle Peter called for repentance so that times of refreshing may come from You, oh God, we say that this generation and the future generations shall be saved from becoming perverse generations.

This generation shall follow the commands of God without grumbling, griping or dissension.

We say that this generation shall prove itself to be blameless and innocent in the eyes of God, above reproach in the midst of perversion. This generation shall appear as a light unto the world, holding fast to the *word of life*. We decree a holy reverence over this generation and its future for the things of God.

Your dominion shall endure over America throughout all generations. For Your Spirit hovers over this Nation. You have anointed America to bring good news to the poor, You have established America so that the brokenhearted may be healed, so that the captives may be set free. This generation and its future will manifest the promises of God over America.

There will be such a turnaround because of their dependence on You, oh God. Ruins shall be rebuilt, waste places repaired, rejoicing instead of confusion, double honor over this Nation, instead of shame!

God, we know that You are able to do exceedingly, abundantly more for this generation and for the preservation of future generations – more than we could ever ask or think about.
                    Ephesians 3:20-21, paraphrased

Let it be so, we pray, in Jesus' name. Amen.

CHILDREN

God thank You that children are a blessing from You. Your Word tells us to train up children in the way they should go and they will never depart from it. First and foremost, Father we pray for the strength, wisdom and discernment for every parent to protect and raise up their children in the ways of the Lord. We dedicate our children of this Nation to You, oh God.

We pray that the blessings of God come to those who love and obey His Word and will flow down on our children and our children's children, even unto the thousandth generation of those who love You. Let not the enemy come into our bloodline and steal the blessings from our children, oh God.

We commit to closing the door to the enemy in the lives of children in this Nation: doors that may have brought trauma at a young age, child abuse, neglect, allowing our children to be raised by TV and electronics rather than by the Spirit of the Lord. Forgive us oh God, when we have not prayed for all children, nor taught them how to pray.

God we ask for restoration of the innocence in the minds, hearts and spirits of our Nation's children, that their mouths would sing forth praise unto You to silence the foe and defeat the enemy as he would try to destroy the generations.

Forgive us for allowing children to be exposed to wickedness in ideas, thoughts, concepts, images and sounds.

Forgive us when we have not been righteous FILTERS, standing in the gap against exposure to wickedness.

Give us strength to stand against the cunning strategies and attacks of the enemy.

The prince of the power of the air would seek to infiltrate the hearts and minds of our children. But we take authority now, and we say the enemy must depart in the name of Jesus. We loose a righteous disdain in the hearts and minds of our children for everything evil. As they see things that are not of God, they would say NO, turn away from it and report it to a parent or adult who can cover them in prayer from infiltration.

Raise up a spirit of perception and holy filtering in adults who will stand up against the onslaught of the enemy upon our Nation's children, in Jesus' name.

We also beseech You, God for the people and facilities who care for our children day by day. God You know the weight of the precious assignment that daycare providers, school staff, after school program personnel and those who work in recreational facilities carry.

Father we pray for righteous and right-minded people to be in these roles, people who will care for the children and not seek to abuse their power over them.

According to Galatians 5:22-23, we pray for the *Fruit of the Spirit* to increase in the lives of these caretakers, that they will, with great diligence and developmental appropriateness, teach and treat these children with love, joy, peace, patience, gentleness, kindness, meekness, faith and self-control.

God, as the children are our future, we pray for a future that is bright, in Jesus' name. Amen.

YOUTH AGES 12 - 17

Father, in the name of Jesus, thank You for the youth of this Nation, that group who in fifty years will be entering their senior years. Even today, we pray that they will not forget the days of their youth, and that their youthful years will be filled with precious, joyous memories. We pray for the youth who are with their biological families, and we especially pray for homeless youth, youth in the Nation's foster care system and youth who have been placed in juvenile correctional systems.

God, please forgive us, those in generations ahead of them, where we have not set high holy standards by which they must live. Help us impart standards that You set. Let us teach our children and the generations following.

Forgive us when we have not trusted You for their lives and instead tried to fill their lives with things of this world.

Please forgive us for turning them over to technology as their teachers instead of taking the time to love, discipline, play with and teach them ourselves. We ask You to restore the years of lost family time.

Give us a chance to renew our vows to our children and grandchildren. Vows to teach them Your ways, to guide them to You, to discipline, but not to harm them, to provide for their good mental, physical and spiritual growth and development, to love them with a righteous parental love.

Father, we decree and declare that all the evil forces that try to draw the youth away from You shall be bound; that no weapon formed against them by the evil one shall prosper; that every tongue that rises up against them, You shall condemn. For You say they are a blessed generation, not the statistic that the world would say.

You say they are the future world leaders who will come into a time not seen by generations before them. They will be a generation of leaders of integrity, of high moral standards, those who are good stewards of the precious earth You have loaned to us.

They will be thoughtful and kind to their parents and not slaves to technology. Father, by the power You have given us, we utterly annihilate the scorpions and serpents that arise against this generation through divorce, abuse, molestation, abandonment, and access to and use of drugs, guns and weapons of mass destruction. We come against bullying, lack of civil discourse, premature death, suicide, apathy, lack of purpose, sexual immorality and spiritual complacency.

Father we come against the spirit of confusion that would question the authority of how You made them – as man or woman.

God, please TEAR ASUNDER the veil of wickedness that would seek to separate this generation from You!

Lord, give our national leaders the courage to move in righteousness with respect to laws and policies that affect this generation. Let them not be swayed by public opinion, but let them seek after what is the best for the young people of the Nation to fulfill their God-ordained purpose in the earth!

We loose Your original intent for their lives and we say COME FORTH as the mighty, righteous, holy, kingdom warriors of the Lord!

"Before I formed you in the womb, I knew you; Before you were born I sanctified you; I ordained you a prophet to the nations."

Then said I: "Ah, Lord God! Behold, I cannot speak for I am a youth." But the Lord said to me; "Do not say I am a youth, for you shall go to all to whom I send you, and whatever I command you, you shall speak.

Do not be afraid of their faces, for I am with you to deliver you," says the Lord.
Jeremiah 1:5-8

YOUNG ADULTS
MILLENNIALS AND GENERATION X

Oh Lord, Your name shall be declared from generation to generation! We decree this for the Millennials and Generation X in this Nation! Thank You, God that You are all knowing, all powerful in the lives of Your people.

We pray, in this era of technological change, to bind the prince of the power of the air off the hearts and minds of these generations. Mighty God, these generations shall live, move and have their being in You, not in technology, not in self, not in the things of this world.

We speak peace over these generations, even as the world would exhibit chaos and confusion. We declare that these generations shall know their God: they shall be Your people and You shall be their God.

We thank You for the Joshuas and Calebs in their midst, those who can see the promises of God in the midst of apparent problems. Thank You for the Esthers in these generations, who are willing to *go before the King* as instructed on behalf of her people with a *nevertheless* attitude about her own outcome, as long as her people shall be saved.

We thank You for the Josephs and the sons of Issachar in these generations, who have been called as prophetic dreamers and seers, who have been placed in strategic positions. They understand the times and know what to do. They shall leverage the anointing on their lives to usher in God's salvation.

We praise You for the Daniels, Hananiahs and Mishaels, whose commitment to You is so strong, God, that they will walk as standard-bearers for the Lord, even in the midst of persecution, danger and death.

We raise up special prayers for African American young men, who have been attacked by oppression, fatherlessness, drugs, alcohol, undiagnosed mental conditions, depression, stressors, rebellion, imprisonment and death. We decree and declare that generational curses must cease, in Jesus' name! We say systemic barriers must be eliminated, in Jesus' name.

We decree and declare that the spirit of the Father will arise in these generations. They shall know the Father of all. Through intimacy with You God, they shall be good fathers.

We pray for the spirit of truth to be released upon them, the truth of who they are in Christ – more than conquerors, a royal priesthood, a holy nation, God's chosen!

We declare that the hand of the enemy must cease to profile, target and fear the young African American. He too is a patriot, a citizen, a lover of country and a man of honor. Thank You God, that the African American man shall be afforded his right due as a man, worthy of respect and full of dignity.

We pray for the entrepreneurial spirit that is alive in so many young African American men to come forth, flourish and find favor with God and man. Thank You God, for the spirit of the faithful father, son and brother that is alive in the hearts of the African American man. Thank You for his strength against the odds, his resilience and his loyalty, even in the face of past betrayals.

We believe for the leadership mantle to arise upon the African American young man. We declare a new day of peace, security and stability in Jesus' name for him and his posterity!

SENIORS

Mighty God, we thank You for the length of days You have shown seniors. As they have turned to You, surely You have promised long life and revealed salvation to those who love and acknowledge You. God, we acknowledge that You can use seniors as much as You can use the young.

We pray that seniors will continue to trust in You even as they did in the days when they first met You. We pray a spirit of Abraham upon them, who did not allow his circumstances or physical conditions to stop him from moving in Your perfect will to become the father of many nations.

Thank You for the renewed understanding that You give

seniors for the work they still can do in the days ahead and to secure the blessings for future generations.

For seniors of this Nation, Lord God, we ask that You would honor them among the Nation, that the wisdom, knowledge and understanding that You gave them would not be pushed aside.

We come against age discrimination, isolation, alienation and loneliness among our seniors. We come against elder abuse, fraudulent activity and scams that would seek to destroy all that our seniors have worked for.

We take authority over abusive medication practices that would come in the deceitful mask of a medical cure, but in reality, *zaps* the life and vitality from our seniors. Revive them in the midst of their years, we pray, and allow our seniors to shine bright among the people of this Nation.

Thank You, Mighty God, for inter-generational connections, between builders and boomers, between boomers and millennials, between millennials and the next generation and across all generations, so that the wisdom of God may be shared abundantly. Please give our young people a spirit of obedience and honor for their elders, and a hunger to learn from them. Let not one thing be left undone in the lives of our seniors, but allow them to finish what You have placed them on the earth to do, in Jesus' name. Amen.

DELIVERANCE FROM OPIOIDS

God, we think about the ease with which these little white pills go down, that causes one to *feel good*; but, there is a hidden disease that creeps up on the lives of those who take them; this is the height of deception which leads to destruction.

God, we pray for relief of pain to come upon people in a way that would not require these opioids. God it was never Your intention for Pharma to take the place of Rapha, Our Healer!

You are The Great I Am, oh God! You are the God who heals us! We pray for an exposure and understanding of the demonic twists and turns that have caused the opioid crisis in this country.

We decree that America's leaders shall speak out against the pharmaceutical companies who care more about the almighty dollar than they care about the health of the people.

We come against deceptive marketing schemes that would promise a joyful life instead of telling the truth about the detrimental side effects that many of these drugs carry. We ask You to give doctors who have taken the Hippocratic Oath – to do no harm, to have the courage to not be hypocrites – to stand up against the marketing schemes and the mammon ploys that would try to get them to sell the health of a society for a fee.

We pray for legislation and regulation of this industry. For we know that while there may be some good in it, without restraint, people have literally perished!

We come against the stigma of the person who is *on* opioids who feels like there is no other way to manage the pain. God, we call for our physicians who are so tied up in the western ways of medicine to look beyond their finite understanding and ask for the divine understanding of God to reveal the ancient ways of healing before these drugs, these chemicals were being used.

We pray for the ancient ways, oh God, oh Ancient of Days, we pray for the ancient wisdom, we pray for the healing of our Nation.

We pray for a smart and effective way for people to wean off these drugs and for them to come into a place of true healing.

No more will the big Pharma lobbyists get their way in the halls of Congress.

No more will there be suggestions for laws and lack of regulations that go unquestioned. No more will the suggestions for the FDA approval of drugs go without deep scrutiny as to the long-term effects each drug could have on the population now and for generations to come. No longer, no longer!

Give Your people, oh God, supernatural strength to overcome this wicked addiction! Send Your angels oh God, into the households, the hospitals, the hallways of government and even the hallowed church pews, to help Your people be set free.

Save Your people from demonic side effects. Lord we pray You save them from suicide and homicide. Let the true demonic impact of these drugs be exposed for what they are! Where families have been devastated by the impact of prescription drugs and the medical malpractice caused by them, let the legal settlements come to pass.

Let Your Glory rise in the church Lord God, that they might operate again in the healing mantle, helping people to be set free. Jehovah Rapha we believe You for this prayer, in Jesus' name. Amen.

CHEMICAL SECTOR

We offer prayers for the chemical sector of our Nation, the sector which produces more than seventy thousand diverse products that have been considered essential to modern life. In several hundred thousand US manufacturing facilities, these chemicals are produced and distributed in a complex, global supply chain.

We first and foremost ask for the forgiveness of the Divine for what our national laws and policies have allowed these facilities and products to do in cities, towns, superfund sites, rivers and springs across this great land. We pray that God would give our Nation's leaders, wisdom as to which products and chemicals, once thought to be essential, must now be discontinued due to hazards to humans, animals and the environment.

God, bring an urgent sense for divine stewardship over the planet to the hearts and minds of this Nation's leaders, for posterity sake. We take authority now, over the god of mammon that would seek profit over the general health and welfare of the people and planet; short-term personal gain over long-term planetary problems and pain.

And we loose a spirit of rightful stewardship over the great natural riches and wealth by which You have blessed this Nation.

We pray for America's leaders to have keen discernment as to how to rightly govern this sector. This complex sector is one that many have seen as a significant provider of the comforts of life in our homes, communities and Nation. Yet, others have seen the problems with pesticides, chemicals and products that have become sources of cancer in humans. Others have seen the low-biodegradable plastics become afflictions to life on land, in drinking water and oceans. Even the breakdown of plastics has become a potential harm to the air, by releasing methane gas.

Oh God, what have the hands of man wrought in the earth! Please forgive us and show us the way out. Many do not want these products regulated, and rightfully so. But regulate the heart of man and his desires for posterity's sake!

(Proverbs 21:1, paraphrased)

God, we pray for researchers and scientists to arise, whose discoveries will bring us closer to harmony and alignment with the natural order of things. Reveal to this new breed of Godly scientists how science can be in sync with the order of God. Allow for the discovery of new products and new ways of operating in this sector that will reverse the damage that has been done and chart a new course for our Nation and the planet, in Jesus' name. Amen.

EMERGENCY SERVICES SECTOR

LAW ENFORCEMENT (POLICE AND SHERIFF DEPARTMENTS), FIRE AND RESCUE SERVICES, EMERGENCY MEDICAL SERVICES, EMERGENCY MANAGEMENT, PUBLIC WORKS; SPECIALIZED CAPABILITIES

Mighty God in the name of Jesus we praise and glorify Your name, we thank You God for our emergency services officials and for those who serve in times of crisis. God even as they seek to provide protection and crisis support for people in need, we pray that You will be their protection. Oh God, be a fortress and strong tower for them!

Oh God, we pray that every person in this system will take refuge in the shadow of Your wings; we pray that though they walk in the midst of trouble, You preserve their life; You stretch out Your hand against the anger of their foes. With Your right hand You save them. We pray that You keep them safe from the hands of the wicked. Protect them from the violent and those who devise ways to trip them up. Mighty God we pray for the hearts of those who are First Responders. Let them be pure-hearted people; people who would not use the vulnerability of others or the authority that You have vested in them to misuse people or situations.

God, we pray right now for justice to reign over this land for surely You are a God of Justice. We thank You God that law enforcement officials and those with special capabilities operate in a spirit of justice and righteousness.

Mighty God, You are our rock and our salvation in whom we trust. We pray, oh God that these officials would call upon You in times of trial for wisdom, discernment and direction. Surely God, You are worthy to be praised.

Mighty God we also *lift up* the fire fighters, 911 dispatchers, hazmat teams and other special units. We pray for a spirit of perseverance to evolve out of all the suffering they see and hear. Out of that endurance, strengthen them in character and give them a hope that would never disappoint (Romans 5:3-5). We pray for the families of First Responders, the husbands, wives and children of those who put their lives on the line every day. Mighty God we pray a hedge of protection around them as they go about their routine.

Father we especially pray for our frontline police officers who go into potential danger every time a call is dispatched. Father we pray for wisdom and discernment for these men and women who have a heart to protect and to serve. We also pray a hedge of protection around their families and their children, that there would be no undue worry or unnecessary concern about the safety and security of their loved ones.

Father we pray that every one of these men and women who go out every day to serve our cities and communities would know that they are working for You. Let their yes be yes, their no be no, and let their hands mete out justice and righteousness.

We take authority over corruption in the law enforcement system in the name of Jesus. We say that every corruption will be exposed and uncovered. Those corrupt people who try to hide behind the shield of law enforcement would be found out, and quickly.

Mighty God we understand the complexities of undercover work and we do pray for those who operate in an undercover capacity. But Mighty God, we pray that those who are operating undercover remember who they are. We pray that they do not get caught up in the evils of the system in which they operate. We thank You for the angels that You encamp around them, keeping them in all their ways that they dash not their foot against a stone. We thank You God that if they call on You, You will bear them up on the shoulders of Your angels.

Mighty God we also pray for improved communication among and between our first responders, law enforcement officials, firefighters, emergency medical technicians, emergency management officials, and all those who are on the front lines in crisis and disaster.

We establish clear communication lines in the spirit realm that would be manifested in the natural realm. We bind confused communications in the name of Jesus. We loose clear communications and say that people will be in the right place at the right time.

FOOD & AGRICULTURAL SECTOR
REGISTERED FOOD MANUFACTURING, PROCESSING AND STORAGE FACILITIES

The fields and streams are Yours, oh God! Purify the hearts and minds of those who work therein. Magnify Your presence in everything that makes its way into the stomach of man from these fields and streams. We are what we eat, Lord, so we pray for farm to table nutrition to be applauded, lauded, promoted, afforded and consumed by Your people once again. We pray for those with the skills and minds to produce fruits and vegetables, to be called upon by the churches, cities and regions to bring people back to an appreciation and proper usage of the fertile lands and streams.

We come against unrighteous agribusiness practices focused on profit instead of the plentifulness of God. We pray for the small farmers, producers and distributors who continue to produce and handle food products according to Your divine principles. Lord, allow them to still profit for their principled practices while making products affordable to the common man. Institute laws and policies that will honor their labor of providing nutritious products to people in Jesus' name.

We come against unrighteous practices in the supplements industry, which have given people a false sense of well-being. Too often people are being sold sugars and fillers. We pray for policies and legislation to regulate *snake oil* salesmen who pilfer the people for unholy profit.

We call a cease and desist order on genetically modified agricultural practices that cause harm and imbalance to the agricultural systems.

We come against deadly counterfeits to the things You created, God!

We come against practices that pervert the nutritional and medicinal value of the world's food supply.

God please take us back to biblical models of eating like Daniel chapter 2. Let us not destroy the future food supply, but teach our progeny Your way of feeding the masses! In Jesus' name.

TRANSPORTATION SYSTEMS SECTOR

Mighty God we thank You in the name of Jesus, that You have given us mobility through various forms of transportation in this Nation. Thank You Mighty God, that the systems in this Nation – which carry millions of passengers and possessions each day are guarded, guided and given by You. God, You have blessed us with these systems that we might have and enjoy greater access to each other, to goods, services and even to other nations. Forgive us when we have taken these sectors for granted and have mistreated the blessing or the people who work, operate and care for them.

AVIATION

Thank You Lord for the aviation sector (public and private). We pray now for every pilot, air traffic controller, aviation mechanic, luggage handler, reservation agent, gate agent, special assistance employees, airport workers, ground transportation providers, rental car agencies, TSA agents, flight attendants, waste handlers, food handlers, radar analysts, navigators and yes Lord, even the custodial and janitorial staff of airport facilities.

Thank You for giving each and every one keen eyesight, insight and foresight. Give them the heart to be alert and aware, even acting as Your *special security and comfort agents* for the millions of passengers they serve each day. Forgive us Mighty God when we have overlooked, taken for granted or misused/abused these people, or negated or minimized their important service and the safety they provide.

We pray for their health, binding all preventable and avoidable occupational hazards and long-term hazardous effects, and we loose stamina, proper circadian rhythm and support for their legs, veins, respiratory and circulatory systems. God please have Your way in their lives, for as these people are alert, aware, healthy and effective, so is the air-travelling public.

Lord thank You for safety and a spirit to *follow the rules* among passengers. We take authority over unruliness, drunkenness, rebellious spirits and haughty, ungrateful, irreverent and disrespectful attitudes. God, we declare that air passengers will see the blessing even with flight delays and safe take-offs and landings, for they do not know or understand everything that those in the aviation sector must deal with.

We speak over airline manufacturers and those who design, build, test and produce these phenomenal flying machines and we thank You God for greater wisdom and revelation to come upon these people, so that the planes can be produced in a more economical and eco-friendly fashion, without compromising safety for profit.

Mighty God, we ask Your blessing over aviation, especially to guard the system against terror, malfunction, accident and human error. We cover it with the blood of Jesus, and we thank You God for allowing man to take flight, like the eagle.

HIGHWAYS, BRIDGES, RAIL LINES AND TUNNELS

Mighty God we lay every road, bridge, rail line and tunnel that has been carved into the face of this land before You. We ask Your forgiveness for those we ignore, and their descendants whose blood, sweat and tears built these passage ways, sometimes even by the sacrifice of human life. Forgive us when we take for granted that a road, bridge, rail line or tunnel is *just there,* not remembering those who went before us and plowed the way.

God, make us proper stewards over this land; allow us to use creative ways to traverse the land without unnecessary loss of life and without unnaturally covering up the surfaces of Mother Earth, the planet.

We take authority over deforestation and cementing, rubbering or laying foreign materials over the surface of the earth – for surely the earth breathes along with us – and we with it – and the natural surface brings balance to the heat of the sun.

God, we do acknowledge and thank You for the passageways that have balanced usefulness to man while avoiding destabilization, desecration and destruction of the planet. God give us greater wisdom for the future creation, maintenance and when necessary, dismantling of the Nation's passageways, in Jesus' name.

MARITIME AND PORTS OF ENTRY

Oh Lord, how excellent is Your name in all the earth! We marvel at the beauty and majesty of Your handiworks, the earth, the sky, the seas, and everything therein. As we glance upon the seas and the places where You allow the waters to meet man on land, we thank You for the numerous ports and maritime passages that You have allowed man to design. In this Nation alone, oh God, we thank You for the hundreds of ports of call, commerce, human passage and gateways to the world that they represent.

We ask that You forgive us, oh God, when we have allowed these ports

to be used for ungodly purposes; whether for trafficking in guns, drugs and people; or human smuggling or being open channels for terror in our cities, states and Nation.

Please God, we pray that You would cover our ports; send Your warring angels to interrupt illegal commerce and activity therein. Please give your port workers, customs and border patrol agents discernment as to what is being transported in those cargo holds, even though they cannot physically inspect every one due to sheer volume. Give them heightened discernment we pray; lead them to those containers that must be stopped. Apprehend the illicit, illegal and ill-intentioned shipments in the name of Jesus!

Please bless our port security staff Lord, and allow these gateways to become filters of righteousness to block out those elements that must not enter in!

PRAYER FOR PASTORS & FAITH LEADERS

Heavenly Father, we lay the pastors and faith leaders in American churches at the foot of Your throne. We cry out for the pastors and faith leaders who are called by Your name to humble themselves, to pray together, to seek Your face. We pray for the church in America to turn from all wickedness!

We repent on behalf of the church in America! Please forgive us when we have not focused on the Great Commission. Please forgive us when the church has been a place of hurt instead of a place of healing. Please forgive us, oh God, when the church has been a place of obligation and bondage, instead of a place of hope and deliverance. Forgive us, oh God, when the church has looked like the world instead of manifesting Your holy Word!

We pray for a spirit of unity to come upon the church in America, for in unity You have commanded a blessing, life forevermore! We ask, oh God, for the church to be one even as You and Christ Jesus are One. Let the church manifest the love of Jesus in the Earth so that the people will know that You sent Jesus to save, to heal, to deliver.

We ask for a kingdom mindset in the church of America. As pastors and faith leaders lead the people to pray Thy kingdom come, Thy will be done, bring them to the knowledge and understanding of what that truly means. We ask for pastors and faith leaders who can mobilize the people whom they have been given to shepherd, to be a spiritual force for the will of God, to do God's work in their sphere of influence in the Nation.

We ask for pastors and faith leaders who are not conformed to this world, but who are transformed by the renewing of their mind. We need pastors and faith leaders who can express and manifest the good, acceptable and perfect will of God to the people of this Nation.

We pray for pastors and faith leaders who will never fear persecution or mocking from a world system for the sake of Christ and the cross! Instead they will continue to raise the standard of the Word of God amongst the people.

We *clothe* our pastors and faith leaders in the full armor of God, so they are able to stand against the subversive elements that seek to eat away at the core message of the Gospel of Jesus. They shall be clothed with the belt of truth, the breastplate of righteousness, their feet shall be covered with the preparation of the gospel of peace, they shall put on the helmet of salvation, they shall carry the shield of faith in one hand and the sword of the spirit in the other.

They shall pray in the Spirit more than they preach. They shall pray to be given power from on high by the Holy Spirit to lead the people and to shift atmospheres in the communities, cities and the Nation where You, oh God, have placed them. They shall not be mouthpieces for the culture of today, but they shall be Your voice, oh God, to let the people know of the mystery of the Gospel, of Your eternal principles, commandments and truth.

They shall lift up the name of Jesus, without compromise, and draw all people unto Him, unto His Word and His ways. They shall not preach to *tickle the ears*, but to convict and transform the very soul of man.

Dear Lord, we ask that You accept this prayer, these declarations on behalf of leaders in the church of America. In Jesus' name. Amen.

(adapted – 2 Chronicles 7:14; Psalm 133:1, 3; John 17:3, 11; Matthew 6:10; Romans 12:2; Matthew 5:11; Ephesians 6:13-18; John 12:32; 2 Timothy 4:3)

THE PROSELYTE'S POETIC PRAYER TO PRESERVE A NATION *ON SHIGIONOTH* (IMPASSIONED TRIUMPH)

We the people united under
Grace
In order to conform to The Perfect
Unity
Repent for our injustice
Intercede for domestic
tranquility
We Cry out to You Lord of Hosts to
defend
We depend
And rend
Our trust at Your throne of
provision
We turn from division
To the blessing of unity
Of liberty for ourselves and for our
children's children
We the pilgrims
Of Your eternal lineage
Do delineate the Gospel Truth
We subdue
The fiery fallacies forged by the father
of lies
We despise

The shame
Fix our eyes
On the Name above all names
We proclaim
Peace
We the priests
Of the most High
Do enter the Holy of Holies day and
night
And make petition for the right
Of all sons and daughters to
prophesy
The promise of Your return Oh Christ
We do solemnly swear
To prepare
The way
For the coming day
When every knee will bow
And every tongue will proclaim
That Jesus Christ is Lord
We the wielders of the Sword
Of the Spirit of Truth
Do hereby conclude
That these United States
Will be a Nation
Who waits
On You
Amen

Baiyina Abdas

NAMES OF GOD

Abba: Father (Mark 14:36)

Adonai: Lord, my Lord (Psalm 8:1)

**Elohim Tzevaot (Sabaoth):
Lord of Hosts** (Joshua 5:14)

Akal 'Esh: Consuming Fire
(Deuteronomy 4:24)

Almighty (2 Corinthians 6:18)

Alpha and Omega
(Revelations 1:18)

El Shaddai: All Sufficient One
(2 Corinthians 9:8)

Ancient of Days (Daniel 7:9)

Anointed One (Messiah) Jesus
(Acts 4:26)

**Author and Finisher of our faith
(Jesus)** (Hebrews 12:1-2)

Author of Eternal Salvation
(Hebrews 5:9)

**Author of Life, Prince of Life
(Jesus)** (Acts 3:15)

Author of Peace
(1 Corinthians 14:33)

Blessed Hope (Titus 2:13)

Branch (Jesus) (Zechariah 6:12)

Bread of Life (John 6:26)

Bright and Morning Star (Revelation 22:16)

Shield and Buckler to all who trust Him (Psalm 18:30)

By Whom all things were made in Heaven and in Earth (John 1:3)

The Word (John 1:1)

The Way, The Truth and The Life (John 14:6)

The Comforter (Holy Spirit) (John 14:26)

Wonderful, Counselor, Everlasting Father Prince of Peace, Our Perfect Peace (Isaiah 9:6)

Creator of the ends of the earth (Isaiah 40:28)

Dayspring from on high (Luke 1:78)

Deliverer (Romans 11:26)

Desire of all nations (Haggai 2:7)

Door (John 10:9)

Sovereign God (1 Timothy 6:15)

The Great I Am (Exodus 3:14)

El Elyon: Most High God
(Psalm 78:56)

El Gibhor: The Mighty God
(Isaiah 9:6)

Elohim: The God of Israel
(Genesis 1, Exodus 3:1)

El Olam: Eternal God
(Genesis 21:33)

El Roi: God who sees
(Genesis 16:33)

Everlasting King (Jeremiah 10:10)

Faithful and True (Jesus)
(Revelation 19:11)

Faithful Creator (1 Peter 4:19)

Faithful Witness (Jesus)
(Revelation 1:5)

Father of Glory (Ephesians 1:17)

Father of Lights (James 1:17)

Father of Mercies
(2 Corinthians 1:3)

Father of the Fatherless
(Psalm 68:5)

Our Spiritual Father (Hebrews 12:9)

Firstborn of all Creation (Jesus)
(Romans 8:29)

Sure Foundation (Isaiah 28:16)

Steadfast Anchor (Hebrews 6:19)

Fountain of Living Waters
(Jeremiah 2:13)

Fullness of the Godhead (Jesus)
(Colossians 2:9)

Glorious Lord (Isaiah 33:21)

God and Father of All
(Ephesians 4:6)

The Word (Logos) made flesh
(John 1:14)

My Maker (Job 35:10)

God of Abraham, Isaac and Jacob
(Exodus 3:6)

God of All Comfort
(2 Corinthians 1:3)

God of All Flesh (Jeremiah 32:27)

God of All Grace (1 Peter 5:10)

God of All Glory (Psalm 29:3)

Revealer of Secrets (Daniel 2:47)

God of Heaven (Daniel 2:44)

ACKNOWLEDGEMENTS

To Bishop Dr. Jackie L. Green, Founder, JGM *E*nternational Prayer Life Institute, whose obedience to the Lord bears much fruit for the Kingdom of God.

To Mother Artherrine Hoskins, Founder, Global Prayer Network, whose tireless vision of one Nation under God provides the impetus for the Monday Night Prayers for the Nation;

To Greater Impact Church, Bishop Alfred & Lady Iris Smith, Apostle Andrae and Prophet Krystal Holland; whose effectual, fervent prayers avail much;

Faithful intercessors and leaders who know how to finish well;

And to the future generations, may these prayers encourage you and bear good fruit upon which you can continue to advance the Kingdom of God.

ABOUT THE AUTHOR

Minister of the Gospel, Strategist, Planner, Advisor, Public Policy Expert — Jannah Scott has served in many capacities with faith, government, business and the nonprofit community. Jannah is passionate about praying for the United States of America, its elected and appointed leaders and the people of this great Nation.

In 1996, Jannah and her family were baptized as believers in Jesus Christ at First Institutional Baptist Church (FIBC) in Phoenix, Arizona. She has served with the JGM *E*nternational Prayer Life Institute for over twenty years. God's assignment on Jannah's life has included ministry to and with people at all levels of society from the homeless, substance abused, abandoned, and neglected; to high-ranking elected and appointed government officials - both in the US and abroad. She is a woman who deeply believes in Jesus, the five-fold ministry offices, and the gifts and operations of the Holy Spirit.

Highlights of Ms. Scott's ministry assignments include: Chaplain, Phoenix Mercury Women's Basketball; PrayerQuake Statewide Prayer Conferences; Associate, International Foundation (host to the annual National Prayer Breakfast); Led the Ministry of Presence effort out of the Arizona Governor's Office in the aftermath of the 2005 hurricanes (Katrina, Rita and Wilma); Interfaith dialogue, engagements and efforts on behalf of the Obama Administration; Advisor to the church uniting team for Greater Impact Church; and currently serves as a preacher, a spiritual ambassador, and a teacher of the Gospel of Jesus.

WATCH FOR ADDITIONAL VOLUMES OF

STANDING ON THE WALL
PRAYERS TO PRESERVE THE INTEGRITY OF A NATION

www.ingramcontent.com/pod-product-compliance
Lightning Source LLC
Chambersburg PA
CBHW060525130626
46553CB00002B/652